Visit Bib

Contents

Note: All Scripture quotations I've included are from the NIV, but feel free to use any translation you prefer.

The Conversion, Ministry, and Death of the Apostle Paul

Sometimes, people need a strong wakeup call before they'll see the light, and Paul is the perfect example. He went from being a hater of Christ to being one of His most famous followers. His conversion and ministry teach us many lessons from the Lord, including how to share our faith and trust God in the face of difficulty.

The lessons I've included in this volume cover Paul's story in the Book of Acts and what we know of his death.

Each of the 11 lessons in this volume has games, crafts, and other activities to help you teach the stories and to help the kids apply the message. I'm also including a list of resources you might want to add to the lessons to make them that much better.

Recommended Extras

You don't need anything extra to use the lessons. I will, however, provide some suggestions you might find helpful. You can use these resources in addition to or instead of the ideas I've provided.

Here are the resources I recommend for the entire series. I'll list story-specific resources at the end of each lesson.

The Complete Illustrated Children's Bible – for telling the stories with beautiful artwork and Biblical accuracy

The Beginner's Bible: Timeless Stories for Children – for telling the stories to younger children

Greatest Heroes and Legends of the Bible: The Apostles –
another animated video with a Disneyesque art style and no
time traveling

Manga Comic Book: Metamorphosis – for your classroom or
church library

My Big Book of Bible Heroes Devotional – a devotional to
recommend for families or older students

Saul Believes in Jesus

Use this children's Sunday School lesson to teach kids about believing in Jesus and sharing our faith with others.

Needed: Bibles

Intro Activity: Christian Story Interview – Have students pair up and ask each other the following questions. They'll then present their partner's answers as a reporter. They can write the answers down if they want.

What is your name?
How old are you?
When did you first hear about Jesus?
When was the first time you went to a church?
When was the first time you came to this church?
What happened to make you start coming to church?
Why do you believe in Jesus?

Lesson: (Note: Always allow students enough time to think about and to give their answers to the questions before clarifying the teaching.)

(Read Acts 9:1-2.)

"Meanwhile, Saul was still breathing out murderous threats against the Lord's disciples. He went to the high priest and asked him for letters to the synagogues in Damascus, so that if he found any there who belonged to the Way, whether men or women, he might take them as prisoners to Jerusalem."

What was Saul going to the city to do? (He was going to arrest all the people who believed in Jesus.)

(Read Acts 9:3-9.)

"As he neared Damascus on his journey, suddenly a light from heaven flashed around him. He fell to the ground and heard a voice say to him, 'Saul, Saul, why do you persecute Me?'

"'Who are you, Lord?' Saul asked.

"'I am Jesus, whom you are persecuting,' He replied. 'Now get up and go into the city, and you will be told what you must do.'

"The men traveling with Saul stood there speechless; they heard the sound but did not see anyone. Saul got up from the ground, but when he opened his eyes he could see nothing. So they led him by the hand into Damascus. For three days he was blind, and did not eat or drink anything."

What happened to Saul that made him change his mind? (He saw a bright light that blinded him, and Jesus talked to him from Heaven.)

Did Saul believe in Jesus after Jesus talked to him? (Yes.)

But you've never heard Jesus talk to you. Can you still believe in Him? (Yes.)

How can you believe in Jesus if you've never heard Him talk to you? (The Bible tells us about Him, and we can feel His Spirit living inside of us.)

(Read Acts 9:10-12.)

"In Damascus there was a disciple named Ananias. The Lord called to him in a vision, 'Ananias!'

"'Yes, Lord,' he answered.

"The Lord told him, 'Go to the house of Judas on Straight Street and ask for a man from Tarsus named Saul, for he is praying. In a vision he has seen a man named Ananias come and place his hands on him to restore his sight.'"

What did Jesus want Ananias to do? (To go see Saul and heal him of his blindness.)

Do you think Ananias would want to go see Saul, or would he be afraid to go see him?

Ananias would probably be afraid to go see Saul because Ananias was a Christian, and Saul was coming to the city to arrest the Christians. Saul was the bad guy.

(Read Acts 9:13-16.)

"'Lord,' Ananias answered, 'I have heard many reports about this man and all the harm he has done to Your holy people in Jerusalem. And he has come here with authority from the chief priests to arrest all who call on Your name.'

"But the Lord said to Ananias, 'Go! This man is my chosen instrument to proclaim my name to the Gentiles and their kings and to the people of Israel. I will show him how much he must suffer for My name.'"

Even though Ananias was afraid to go see Saul, did Jesus still wanted him to do it? (Yes.)

Some things scare us, too, just like Ananias was scared. But Jesus wants us to be brave and do things that are scary sometimes. Remember that Jesus can help us against anything that we're afraid of.

(Read Acts 9:17-22.)

"Then Ananias went to the house and entered it. Placing his hands on Saul, he said, 'Brother Saul, the Lord—Jesus, who appeared to you on the road as you were coming here—has sent me so that you may see again and be filled with the Holy Spirit.' Immediately, something like scales fell from Saul's eyes, and he could see again. He got up and was baptized, and after taking some food, he regained his strength.

"Saul spent several days with the disciples in Damascus. At once he began to preach in the synagogues that Jesus is the Son of God. All those who heard him were astonished and asked, 'Isn't he the man who raised havoc in Jerusalem among those who call on this name? And hasn't he come here to take them as prisoners to the chief priests?' Yet Saul grew more and more powerful and baffled the Jews living in Damascus by proving that Jesus is the Messiah."

What did Saul do after he believed in Jesus and was healed of his blindness? (He started preaching and telling other people to believe in Jesus.)

Do you think God wants us to tell other people about Jesus too? (Yes.)

Since we believe in Jesus, we should tell other people about Him so that they can believe in Jesus and go to Heaven when they die.

Game: Saul Sees the Light –Tell the students that they are going to pretend to be Saul. Tell them to spread out and act like they are walking to the city to arrest all the Christians.

Dim the lights and tell the students that when you turn on the light, they have to pretend that Jesus is appearing to them and get down on their knees as fast as possible and shout, "I believe!"

The person who kneels the fastest gets to control the light next.

6

Game: Disciple Tag – Choose one student to be It. When they tag someone, that person links hands with them and joins their team. They continue adding people to their team, linking hands with each one until all but one student is part of their chain. That remaining student becomes It for the next round.

Play two or three rounds and then, explain that when we tell people about Jesus, we want them to believe in Jesus too. If they do, they become a Christian and join our team. Then, they help us tell more people about Jesus.

Closing Prayer: Jesus, we thank You for appearing to Saul and helping him to believe in You. We thank You that we can believe in You too. Now, help us to share our faith in You with other people. Amen.

Recommended Extras

Superbook: The Road to Damascus – an animated video from the updated Superbook series, includes time-traveling children who learn lessons from the story

Saul Hurts God's People – free coloring and activity pages

> http://freesundayschoolcurriculum.weebly.com/upload
> s/1/2/5/0/12503916/lesson_81_saul_hurts_gods_peopl
> e.pdf

The Apostles Forgive Saul

Use this children's Sunday School lesson to teach students about forgiving others.

Needed: Bibles, To Forgive or Not to Forgive cards, writing or drawing paper, pencils, crayons or colored pencils

Intro Game: Saul the Persecutor – Divide students into two teams. One team is the Christians, and the other team is the Persecutors. Choose one member of the Persecutors to be Saul.

Saul directs the Persecutors to chase a certain Christian. When they tag a Christian, the Christian is out.

The game is over when only one Christian is left. Have the teams switch roles. The last Christian who was left in the game becomes Saul.

Lesson: Ask students, Has anyone ever done something wrong to you?

Is it ever hard to forgive someone when they do something wrong to you?

Last time, we met Saul, who was going to the city to arrest anyone who believed in Jesus. But then, Jesus talked to Saul from Heaven, and instead of hating Jesus and everyone who believed in Jesus, Saul started believing in Jesus himself! Now, let's see what happened next in Saul's life.

(Read Acts 9:20-23.)

"At once he began to preach in the synagogues that Jesus is the Son of God. All those who heard him were astonished and asked, 'Isn't he the man who raised havoc in Jerusalem among those who call on this name? And hasn't he come here to take them as prisoners to the chief priests?' Yet Saul grew more and more powerful and baffled the Jews living in Damascus by proving that Jesus is the Messiah.

"After many days had gone by, there was a conspiracy among the Jews to kill him,"

When Saul started preaching about Jesus, what did the Jewish people want to do to him? (Kill him.)

Why do you think they wanted to kill him for talking about Jesus? (They didn't believe in Jesus and wanted to keep everyone else from believing in Him too.)

Back then, it was illegal to believe in Jesus. It's still that way in many countries today. It is illegal to believe in Jesus, and people are still being put in jail or being killed for believing in Jesus.

(Read Acts 9:24-25.)

"but Saul learned of their plan. Day and night they kept close watch on the city gates in order to kill him. But his followers took him by night and lowered him in a basket through an opening in the wall."

How did Saul escape from the Jewish people? (Other disciples of Jesus lowered him out of the city in a basket, and he ran away.)

(Read Acts 9:26.)

"When he came to Jerusalem, he tried to join the disciples, but they were all afraid of him, not believing that he really was a disciple."

When Saul met the other disciples of Jesus, like Peter, did they trust him? (No.)

Why not? (They remembered that Saul used to be one of the people who was trying to kill them. They were afraid of him and thought that maybe he was just tricking them so that he could arrest them.)

(Read Acts 9:27-28.)

"But Barnabas took him and brought him to the apostles. He told them how Saul on his journey had seen the Lord and that the Lord had spoken to him, and how in Damascus he had preached fearlessly in the name of Jesus. So Saul stayed with them and moved about freely in Jerusalem, speaking boldly in the name of the Lord."

Did the other followers of Jesus eventually trust Saul? (Yes.)

Sometimes, it's hard for us to trust someone again when they do wrong things to us, but as followers of Jesus, we have to forgive people for their wrong things and be willing to give them another chance.

Game: To Forgive or Not to Forgive – Print out or write the words Forgive or Don't Forgive on a set of index cards. You should have an equal number of cards that say Forgive as Don't Forgive.

Divide students into two teams, and have the teams line up on separate sides of the room in single file lines. Mix up the cards and give each student a card that says Forgive or Don't Forgive. Set a timer for 3-5 minutes, depending on how many students you have. When you say, "Go!" the first two students run toward each and show each other their cards.

If one says Forgive and the other says Don't Forgive, the student with Forgive scores a point for their team. The person with Don't Forgive does not score. If both say Forgive, both score a point and if both say Don't Forgive, neither does. Both return to the back of their lines and trade their cards for a new card.

As soon as they leave the center, the second two players run up and do the same thing. Play continues until the timer runs out. The team with the most points at the end wins.

Craft: The Persecuted Church – Look up a current news story about where Christians are being persecuted. Show the location on a map and summarize the situation for the children and explain why a certain government doesn't want the people to believe in God. Then, have students write a prayer for their fellow Christians in that situation, or draw a picture illustrating God's protection around those persecuted Christians.

https://www.opendoorsusa.org/

Closing Prayer: Father God, help us to forgive other people who have wronged us and help us to remember to pray for people who are being persecuted because they believe in You. In Jesus' name we pray, amen.

Recommended Extra

Friends Help Saul Get Away – free coloring and activity pages

http://freesundayschoolcurriculum.weebly.com/upload s/1/2/5/0/12503916/lesson_82_friends_help_paul_get _away.pdf

Saul Strikes Bar-Jesus Blind for Trying to Stop Someone from Believing in Jesus

Use this children's Sunday School lesson to teach kids about listening for and listening to God's voice.

Needed: Bibles, blindfolds, drawing paper, crayons or colored pencils

Intro Activity: Listening for God – Have students find a partner. Blindfold one partner, spin them around, and walk them to somewhere else in the room. When you say "Go!" their partners call their names. The blindfolded partner tries to make it back to the caller.

When all the blindfolded students make it back to their partner, have them switch roles.

Play again if time permits, but make the students find a new partner for each round.

Remind students that we have to listen closely if we want to hear God speaking to us.

Lesson: Ask students, Do you think it's easy to believe in God or not easy to believe in God?

There are a lot of people who don't believe in God. What do you think are some reasons people don't believe in God: (Suggestions could include the fact that we can't see God, they don't know about God, they believe in something else, etc.)

Sometimes, people don't want to believe in God because if they did, they would have to listen to Him and follow His rules, and some people don't want to follow the rules.

(Read Acts 13:1-2.)

"Now in the church at Antioch there were prophets and teachers: Barnabas, Simeon called Niger, Lucius of Cyrene, Manaen (who had been brought up with Herod the tetrarch) and Saul. While they were worshiping the Lord and fasting, the Holy Spirit said, 'Set apart for Me Barnabas and Saul for the work to which I have called them.'"

The Holy Spirit chose Barnabas and Saul to go tell other people about Jesus. Do you think God has chosen you for something? Do you think God could give you a special job like He gave to Barnabas and Saul? (Yes!)

We just have to remember to ask God and pay attention to find out what important job God wants us to do.

(Read Acts 13:3-6.)

"So after they had fasted and prayed, they placed their hands on them and sent them off.

"The two of them, sent on their way by the Holy Spirit, went down to Seleucia and sailed from there to Cyprus. When they arrived at Salamis, they proclaimed the word of God in the Jewish synagogues. John was with them as their helper.

"They traveled through the whole island until they came to Paphos. There they met a Jewish sorcerer and false prophet named Bar-Jesus,"

Who was Bar-Jesus? (A magician and false-prophet.)

That means he pretended to be a leader who could teach people about God, but he was just lying and tricking people with his magic tricks. He wasn't really a teacher from God.

(Read Acts 13:7-8.)

"who was an attendant of the proconsul, Sergius Paulus. The proconsul, an intelligent man, sent for Barnabas and Saul because he wanted to hear the word of God. But Elymas the sorcerer (for that is what his name means) opposed them and tried to turn the proconsul from the faith."

When Saul and Barnabas tried to tell the Governor about Jesus, what did Bar-Jesus do? (He tried to get the governor not to believe in Jesus.)

(Read Acts 13:9-11.)

"Then Saul, who was also called Paul, filled with the Holy Spirit, looked straight at Elymas and said, 'You are a child of the devil and an enemy of everything that is right! You are full of all kinds of deceit and trickery. Will you never stop perverting the right ways of the Lord? Now the hand of the Lord is against you. You are going to be blind for a time, not even able to see the light of the sun.'

"Immediately mist and darkness came over him, and he groped about, seeking someone to lead him by the hand."

What did Saul do to Bar-Jesus for trying to get the Governor to not believe in Jesus? (Saul told Bar-Jesus he was a follower of the devil and not God and made him blind.)

How do you think Saul got the power to make Bar-Jesus blind? (God gave him the power through the Holy Spirit.)

(Read Acts 13:12.)

"When the proconsul saw what had happened, he believed, for he was amazed at the teaching about the Lord."

Saul and Barnabas helped the Governor believe in Jesus. Do you think God wants you to help people believe in Jesus? (Yes.)

Just like Saul and Barnabas, God wants us all to help tell people about Jesus so that they can believe in Jesus and go to Heaven when they die.

Game: Disciple Tag – Choose one student to be It. When they tag someone, that person links hands with them and joins their team. They continue adding people to their team, linking hands with each one until all but one student is part of their chain. That remaining student becomes It for the next round.

Play two or three rounds and then, explain that when we tell people about Jesus, we want them to believe in Jesus too. If they do, they become a Christian and join our team. Then, they help us tell more people about Jesus.

Craft: Learning to Listen – Give students drawing paper and instruct them to draw three scenes of them listening to God. They can then add more paper to their project to make a journal. Instruct them to write down any prayers that they say to God or anything that God says to them in church, through the Bible, or through their prayer time.

Closing Prayer: Holy Spirit, help us listen for Your voice guiding us, just like Paul and Barnabas did. Help us to follow what You say and to help other people believe in You. In Jesus' name we pray, amen.

Paul Is Not a God and Tells Other People to Believe in the Real God

Use this children's Sunday School lesson to teach kids that there is only God.

Needed: Bibles, empty bags or boxes with pictures of various gods taped on them, one blank bag or box with cookies or another prize inside

Intro Game: What's in Box #? – Before class, print out pictures of various gods and paste one picture onto each box or paper bag. Leave one box or bag blank but put a snack or other prize inside to share with the group.

Tell students that you're going to ask for volunteers to come up. You're going to ask them a question, and if they get the answer right, they'll be able to choose one of the boxes or bags. Each of the boxes or bags represents a different god. There might be a prize in the box or bag that they choose.

If a student answers correctly, let them choose a box or bag. If they don't answer correctly, have them sit down and repeat the question for the next volunteer. If the next volunteer doesn't know the answer, review the information with the class and move onto the next question.

When students open all the boxes or bags and discover that only the blank one had anything in it, explain that the blank one represents the real God. We don't know what God looks like, so we can't make a picture of Him. In fact, one of the Ten Commandments is that we should never try to make a picture of God.

But God is the only real God, so He's the only that can give us anything good. That's why only His box/bag had a prize in it.

Lesson: Ask students, Because we are Christians, because we believe in God and Jesus when other people do not, does that make us more special or more important than other people that don't believe in God?

We are not more special or more important than other people. God loves everyone. We're just lucky that we know the truth and that we do believe in Him.

Are pastors or priests more special or more important than the rest of the people in the church?

Pastors and priests are not more special or more important. It's simply that God has given them that special job in the church, and He gives the rest of us other special jobs in the church.

(Read Acts 14:8-10.)

"In Lystra there sat a man who was lame. He had been that way from birth and had never walked. He listened to Paul as he was speaking. Paul looked directly at him, saw that he had faith to be healed and called out, 'Stand up on your feet!' At that, the man jumped up and began to walk."

How did Paul heal the crippled man and make him walk? (God gave him power through the Holy Spirit.)

What did the man need to have to be healed? (He had to have faith. He had to believe in Jesus.)

Game: Get Up! – Have students lie down on the floor. Sitting is fine if you don't have enough room for everyone to lie down. When you yell, "Get up!" everyone should get to their feet and jump into the air as quickly as they can. The first person to jump gets to be the next caller. Play as long as time allows. Be sure to give everyone a chance to be the caller, even if you have to ask someone who's already done it to give up their turn.

(Read Acts 14:11-12.)

"When the crowd saw what Paul had done, they shouted in the Lycaonian language, 'The gods have come down to us in human form!' Barnabas they called Zeus, and Paul they called Hermes because he was the chief speaker."

When Paul healed the man, what did the people think Paul was? (A god.)

Was Paul a god? (No, he was a regular human, like us.)

(Read Acts 14:13-20.)

"The priest of Zeus, whose temple was just outside the city, brought bulls and wreaths to the city gates because he and the crowd wanted to offer sacrifices to them.

"But when the apostles Barnabas and Paul heard of this, they tore their clothes and rushed out into the crowd, shouting: 'Friends, why are you doing this? We too are only human, like you. We are bringing you good news, telling you to turn from these worthless things to the living God, who made the heavens and the earth and the sea and everything in them. In the past, He let all nations go their own way. Yet He has not left Himself without testimony: He has shown kindness by giving you rain from heaven and crops in their seasons; He provides you with plenty of food and fills your hearts with joy.' Even with these words, they had difficulty keeping the crowd from sacrificing to them.

"Then some Jews came from Antioch and Iconium and won the crowd over. They stoned Paul and dragged him outside the city, thinking he was dead. But after the disciples had gathered around him, he got up and went back into the city. The next day he and Barnabas left for Derbe."

Why did the people try to kill Paul? (Because he told them to believe in the real God and not in fake gods.)

How many Gods does the Bible say there are? (One.)

There is only one God. There are three parts to God–God the Father, God the Son (Jesus), and God the Holy Spirit–but they are all one God.

Activity: Acting It Out – Remind students that Paul was able to heal the man who was crippled not because he was more special or more important than other Christians but because God gave Him a special job to do as an apostle.

Ask students, What do you think God could choose you to do for Him? (Write their answers on a blackboard, whiteboard, or a large piece of paper.)

Divide students into groups of two or three. Have each group decide on and act out a scene in which one or two are performing one of the tasks the group mentioned in a way that either benefits other Christians or helps reach out to unbelievers.

Closing Prayer: Father, Son, and Holy Spirit, You are the only one true God. Help us to believe in You and only You and to use our talents to help other people believe in You. Amen.

Jesus Helps Us Get Along with People Who Are Different From Us!

Use this children's Sunday School lesson to teach kids about the unity we have in Christ.

Needed: vegetable oil, vinegar, tablespoon, liquid dishwashing soap, jars with lids, balls or paper wads, "basketball hoops"

Intro Game: If You… – This game is similar to Upset the Fruits Basket. Students sit in a circle with one less chair than players. The person without a chair stands in the middle of the circle and names something that some of the players might have in common.

They might say something like, "If you've never worn a pink sock…" Or, "If you've ever ridden on a plane…" Or, "If you have brown hair." Anyone sitting down who matches what the person in the middle says has to get up and run to a different chair. The person in the middle also tries to find an empty chair. Whoever doesn't find a seat is in the middle.

At the end, comment about how the students all had a lot of things in common and a lot of things that weren't in common.

Lesson: The following lesson is based on Acts 15:1-35.

Ask students, What are some ways that one person could be like another person? What kinds of things could people have in common? (Suggestions could include hobbies, country, religion, race, social class, etc.)

How could people be different? (Again, try to use some of the more obvious divisions.)

Do people usually get along better with people who are like them or people who are different from them?

(Divide students into groups of four and give each group a jar with a lid, a cup of vegetable oil, a cup of vinegar, a cup of dishwashing soap, and a tablespoon.

Everyone, pour half of the vegetable oil into the jar. We're going to pretend that we're like this oil.

Pour the other half of the vegetable oil into the jar. Put the lid tightly on the jar and shake the jar around.

What happened to the first and second halves of oil? Did they mix together or not? (All the oil mixed together.)

When we find other people that are like us, we get along and mix really well together, just like the oil mixed with the other oil because it was the same.

Now, we're going to add some vinegar to the jar, and vinegar is not like oil. What do you think will happen?

Everyone, put a tablespoon of vinegar into the jar. Then, put the lid back on and shake it up.

What happened to the oil and vinegar? (The two didn't mix.)

When we meet someone who is different from us, we might think, "This person is just too different from us," like the vinegar is different from the oil, and we might decide that we don't like that person because they're different.

But Jesus tells us that is not the kind of attitude we're supposed to have. Jesus wants to clean us from having bad thoughts about other people, and He wants us all to get along, even if we are different.

So, everyone, add some of the soap, replace the lid, and shake the jar the around.

What happened this time? (The oil and vinegar mixed together.)

Jesus cleans us our thoughts and attitudes, like soap cleans our bodies, and helps us all to get along.

Jesus' first followers, people like Peter and Paul, had to learn this lesson early on. Jesus was born in the country of Israel, and the people who live in that country are called Jews. Jesus and Peter and Paul were all Jews, and most Jews didn't really like people from other countries. And most people from other countries didn't really like the Jews.

But even though Jesus was a Jew, He didn't come to save only the Jews, did He? No, God loves everyone, not only the Jews! And Jesus wants to save everyone in the whole world, not only the Jews!

That's why Jesus told us that we have to be nice to everyone and tell everyone about Jesus, not only the people who are like us. We have to get along with everyone because God loves everyone, and so that we can tell everyone about how Jesus wants to save them.

Game: Neighbors and Enemies Basketball – Set up two basketball hoops. If you don't have basketball hoops, you can use buckets, trashcans, or boxes to catch the balls. If you have a large group, you can split the students into two or more groups and set up two "baskets" for each group.

One by one, students come up to shoot two balls. They have to shoot one ball at Basket A and the other at Basket B. If they get a basket in each, they score a point. If they get a basket in only one, or neither of the baskets, they do not score a point.

Play long enough for each student to have three turns.

At the end, explain to students that they had to make a basket in each because God wants us to love people who are like us and people who are different from us. We need to treat both the same, just like they had to make a basket in each hoop.

Game: If You… - Play the intro game again and remind students that it's okay to have things in common with people and that it's also okay to have things you don't have in common with people.

Closing Prayer: Lord, we pray that You'll help us to love all people the same, just as You want us to. Clean our attitudes and help us not to think bad thoughts about anyone who is different from us. Amen.

Paul and Barnabas Have a Fight

Use this children's Sunday School lesson to teach kids about how to handle differences they have with someone.)

Needed: Bibles, To Forgive or Not to Forgive cards

Intro Game: If You... – This game is similar to Upset the Fruits Basket. Students sit in a circle with one less chair than players. The person without a chair stands in the middle of the circle and names something that some of the players might have in common.

They might say something like, "If you've never worn a pink sock..." Or, "If you've ever ridden on a plane..." Or, "If you have brown hair." Anyone sitting down who matches what the person in the middle says has to get up and run to a different chair. The person in the middle also tries to find an empty chair. Whoever doesn't find a seat is in the middle.

At the end, comment about how the students all had a lot of things in common and a lot of things that weren't in common. One of the things we have in common with people is when we agree on something. When we disagree about something, that's a difference we have with them.

Lesson: Ask students, Have you ever had a fight with one of your friends? (Invite them to share their stories. The teacher should also share a story.)

Can two people have a fight and both of them be right? (Simply listen to their answers at this point.)

Can two people who both love God have a fight about something? (Again, simply listen to their answers.)

(Read Acts 15:36.)

"Some time later Paul said to Barnabas, 'Let us go back and visit the believers in all the towns where we preached the word of the Lord and see how they are doing.'"

What did Paul want to do? (He wanted to go back to all the churches they had started to see how the people were doing.)

(Read Acts 15:37-38.)

"Barnabas wanted to take John, also called Mark, with them, but Paul did not think it wise to take him, because he had deserted them in Pamphylia and had not continued with them in the work."

What problem did Paul and Barnabas have? (Barnabas wanted to take John Mark on the journey with them, but Paul did not.)

Why didn't Paul want to take John-Mark with them? (When Paul and Barnabas were starting the churches before, John Mark left them and went home. Paul thought that John Mark would leave them again if they took him.)

Why do you think Barnabas wanted to take John Mark with them? (Barnabas wanted to give John Mark a second chance. He thought maybe John Mark would do better this time.)

(Read Acts 15:39-41.)

"They had such a sharp disagreement that they parted company. Barnabas took Mark and sailed for Cyprus, but Paul chose Silas and left, commended by the believers to the grace of the Lord. He went through Syria and Cilicia, strengthening the churches."

Did Paul and Barnabas talk about it and finally come to an agreement? (No. They disagreed with each other and got angry and left, both going their separate ways.)

Does anyone know what John Mark did later in his life? (John Mark wrote the first story of Jesus' life, the book of the Bible we call "Mark.")

Even though Paul and Barnabas had a disagreement, do you think both of them could still do good work for God? (Yes.)

Even though they disagreed, God continued to use both of them to start new Christian churches.

Do you think it's okay for you to have a disagreement with someone sometimes? (Yes.)

We can disagree with people, but we have to remember to keep our tempers under control and not hit or call names or anything like that. We simply need to understand people will not always agree with us and make the same decisions we do. God can still love and be friends with and use both people to do His work.

Game: To Forgive or Not to Forgive – Explain that when we disagree with someone, that doesn't mean we need to be angry with them. We can forgive our differences and still be friends.

Print out or write the words Forgive or Don't Forgive on a set of index cards. You should have an equal number of cards that say Forgive as Don't Forgive.

Divide students into two teams, and have the teams line up on separate sides of the room in single file lines. Mix up the cards and give each student a card that says Forgive or Don't Forgive. Set a timer for 3-5 minutes, depending on how many students you have. When you say, "Go!" the first two students run toward each and show each other their cards.

If one says Forgive and the other says Don't Forgive, the student with Forgive scores a point for their team. The person with Don't Forgive does not score. If both say Forgive, both score a point and if both say Don't Forgive, neither does. Both return to the back of their lines and trade their cards for a new card.

As soon as they leave the center, the second two players run up and do the same thing. Play continues until the timer runs out. The team with the most points at the end wins.

Activity: Acting It Out – Explain that one difference Christians with other Christians is the kind of church that they go to. People might do things differently in those churches, and all Christians don't agree on everything, but that doesn't mean we can't work together to do what God wants us to do.

Divide students into groups of three or four. Have each group decide on and act out a scene in which a group of Christians from other churches can work together to do something.

Closing Prayer: Father God, help us to remember that it's okay to disagree with someone, but help us to forgive those differences and not let them stop the good work that You want us to do. In Jesus' name we pray, amen.

Who to Tell

Use this children's Sunday School lesson to teach kids about when and how to tell others about Christ.

Needed: Bibles, blindfold

Intro Game: Disciple Tag – Choose one student to be It. When they tag someone, that person links hands with them and joins their team. They continue adding people to their team, linking hands with each one until all but one student is part of their chain. That remaining student becomes It for the next round.

Play two or three rounds and then, explain that when we tell people about Jesus, we want them to believe in Jesus too. If they do, they become a Christian and join our team. Then, they help us tell more people about Jesus.

Intro Activity: Acting It Out – Divide students into groups of two or three. Have each group decide on and act out a scene in which someone is sharing about Jesus, but the other person doesn't want to hear it. Ask them to show how each person might react.

Lesson: Ask students, Have any of you ever told somebody about God or Jesus?

What made you want to tell that person about God or Jesus?

What happened when you told them about God or Jesus?

(Read Acts 16:6-10.)

"Paul and his companions traveled throughout the region of Phrygia and Galatia, having been kept by the Holy Spirit from preaching the word in the province of Asia. When they came to the border of Mysia, they tried to enter Bithynia, but the Spirit of Jesus would not allow them to. So they passed by Mysia and went down to Troas. During the night Paul had a vision of a man of Macedonia standing and begging him, 'Come over to Macedonia and help us.' After Paul had seen the vision, we got ready at once to leave for Macedonia, concluding that God had called us to preach the gospel to them."

The Bible tells us that Paul and his friends were traveling in one area, telling people about Jesus, but that the Holy Spirit had told them not to go to Asia or to certain other parts of their country. Why do you think the Holy Spirit would tell them not to go somewhere to tell the people living there about Jesus?

Sometimes, God doesn't want us to tell people about Jesus because maybe they're not ready to believe in Jesus yet. You can tell people about Jesus, but if they're not ready to believe in Him in their hearts, it won't matter what you say.

What did Paul see that night when he was dreaming? (Paul saw a vision of a man in another city asking for help.)

What do you think the man wanted Paul to do to help him? (The man wanted Paul to come to talk to him about Jesus so that he could believe in Jesus and be saved and go to Heaven.)

Did Paul go to help the man? (Yes.)

Do you think God wants you to help people by telling them about Jesus so that they can be saved and go to Heaven when they die? (Yes.)

Game: Who Does God Want You to Talk To? – Pick one student to be It. Put a blindfold on them. Then, silently pick another student to be the Speaker.

Students, including the Speaker, spread out around the room. Then, the Speaker says, "Help me," as quietly or as loudly as they want while the rest of the students talk and make noise. The student who is It has to guess which student the Speaker is.

When It guesses correctly, the Speaker becomes It, and the teacher chooses a new student to be the Speaker. Play until all of the students have had a chance to fill both roles. At the end, explain that we have to listen closely for God to tell who He wants us to talk to about Jesus.

Activity: Acting It Out part 2 – Now, have the groups continue their same scene in which the Christian comes back later, and the other person is ready to listen, or in which the non-Christian later approaches the Christian for more information.

Closing Prayer: Holy Spirit, help us to listen to You to tell us which people to talk to about Jesus and which people not to. In Jesus' name we pray, amen.

Paul Makes a Demon Leave a Girl and Helps a Jailer Believe in Jesus

Use this children's Sunday School lesson to teach kids how God can bring good things out of bad situations.

Needed: Bibles, cookie ingredients and cookies

Intro Activity #1: Complaining Communication – The leader starts off telling a fictitious story about something bad that happened. The students' goal is to then think about all the good things that might have happened afterward.

An example might be, "I went to the fair the other day and dropped my ice cream cone."

The students could then add, "But the ice cream vendor saw what happened and gave me a new ice cream cone for free. Then, someone stole a lady's purse, but the thief slipped on my spilled ice cream, and the police caught him. One of the people who saw it was an old friend of one of the police officers. They hadn't seen each other in years, but when the person saw the police officer arresting the thief, they gave each other their phone numbers. Another person…"

Let kids be as imaginative as possible and ask them questions to prompt their creativity. The only point of the game is to think of how good things outweigh the negative in most situations.

Intro Activity #2: Delicious from Disgusting – Show students a raw egg. Ask them if anyone would like to eat it. Do the same with some raw flour and then baking soda. When no one wants to try any of your ingredients, say, You're right. These would all taste pretty bad if we ate them like this. But we can use them to make something really good! They're all part of the recipe to make cookies. (Give the students a cookie or two as you start the lesson.)

Lesson: Read Acts 16:16-18.

"Once when we were going to the place of prayer, we were met by a female slave who had a spirit by which she predicted the future. She earned a great deal of money for her owners by fortune-telling. She followed Paul and the rest of us, shouting, 'These men are servants of the Most High God, who are telling you the way to be saved.' She kept this up for many days. Finally Paul became so annoyed that he turned around and said to the spirit, 'In the name of Jesus Christ I command you to come out of her!' At that moment the spirit left her."

What did the girl have inside of her? (A spirit.)

What kind of spirit do you think it was? (A demon.)

What is a demon? (A demon is a bad spirit.)

How did Paul make the demon come out of the girl? (He said to the demon, 'In the name of Jesus Christ, I command you to come out of her.')

Because Paul had faith in Jesus, Jesus made the demon come out and leave the girl alone.

(Read Acts 16:19.)

"When her owners realized that their hope of making money was gone, they seized Paul and Silas and dragged them into the marketplace to face the authorities."

Why were the girl's owners angry at Paul?

Paul made the demon go away, which meant that the girl couldn't tell people their fortunes anymore. The demon used to pretend to tell people their future, and people would pay the girl's owners to hear it. The girl's owners were mad now because people wouldn't pay them anymore since the girl couldn't tell them their fortune anymore.

Do you think the girl's owners cared about her, or did they only care about making money? (They only cared about making money. They didn't mind that the girl had a demon living inside her.)

Do you think Paul cared about the girl? (Yes. He made the demon leave the girl so that she would be better.)

(Read Acts 16:20-24.)

"They brought them before the magistrates and said, 'These men are Jews, and are throwing our city into an uproar by advocating customs unlawful for us Romans to accept or practice.'

"The crowd joined in the attack against Paul and Silas, and the magistrates ordered them to be stripped and beaten with rods. After they had been severely flogged, they were thrown into prison, and the jailer was commanded to guard them carefully. When he received these orders, he put them in the inner cell and fastened their feet in the stocks."

Why were Paul and Silas put in jail? (Because they were telling people to believe in the real God instead of fake gods.)

(Read Acts 16:25.)

"About midnight Paul and Silas were praying and singing hymns to God, and the other prisoners were listening to them."

What were Paul and Silas doing during the night? (They were singing and praying to God.)

What do you think they were praying about? (Maybe that the people would believe in Jesus, maybe that God would help them get out of jail, maybe thanking God for giving Paul the power to make the demon leave the girl, etc.)

(Read Acts 16:26.)

"Suddenly there was such a violent earthquake that the foundations of the prison were shaken. At once all the prison doors flew open, and everyone's chains came loose."

What happened to free Paul and Silas? (An earthquake started, and then, all of the prison doors opened, and their chains fell off.)

Who do you think made the earthquake happen? (God. God sent the earthquake to get Paul and Silas out of jail.)

(Read Acts 16:27.)

"The jailer woke up, and when he saw the prison doors open, he drew his sword and was about to kill himself because he thought the prisoners had escaped."

Why do you think the jailer was going to kill himself?

In those days, if you were supposed to be guarding someone and they escaped, you would be killed for letting them escape. The jailer was going to kill himself because he thought he was going to be killed anyway for letting the prisoner's escape.

(Read Acts 16:28.)

"But Paul shouted, 'Don't harm yourself! We are all here!'"

Why do you think Paul and Silas didn't run away when they had the chance? (They stayed because they didn't want the jailer to get killed for them escaping.)

(Read Acts 16:29-34.)

"The jailer called for lights, rushed in and fell trembling before Paul and Silas. He then brought them out and asked, 'Sirs, what must I do to be saved?'

"They replied, 'Believe in the Lord Jesus, and you will be saved—you and your household.' Then they spoke the word of the Lord to him and to all the others in his house. At that hour of the night the jailer took them and washed their wounds; then immediately he and all his household were baptized. The jailer brought them into his house and set a meal before them; he was filled with joy because he had come to believe in God—he and his whole household."

When the jailer saw that the prisoners were all there, he believed in God because he knew that God had sent the earthquake to get Paul and Silas out of jail. What did he ask Paul and Silas then? (He asked how he could be saved.)

And what did Paul and Silas tell the jailer when he asked how he could be saved? (They told him to believe in Jesus.)

If we believe in Jesus, God forgives us for our sins, and we get to go to Heaven and be with God forever when we die.

So, what were the bad things that happened in this story? (Paul and Silas got arrested for teaching about Jesus.)

What were the good things that happened in this story? (Paul made the demon leave the girl, and the jailer believed in Jesus.)

Would the jailer have had a chance to believe in Jesus if Paul and Silas hadn't been arrested? (No.)

So, God used the bad situation of Paul and Silas being arrested to save the jailer and his family.

Game: Jail Tag – Designate an area to be the jail and pick one student to be It. They are the Jailer. The rest of the students are Paul and Silas. The Jailer must tag the rest of the students.

When the Jailer tags them, the students go to jail, just like Paul and Silas did. The leader may pick more than one student to be the Jailer if the Jailer is having a hard time tagging everyone.

Every once in a while or whenever everyone has been caught, the leader calls out "Earthquake!" and the students in the jail are freed and re-enter the game. Rotate students to be the Jailer so that one student doesn't get too tired.

Closing Prayer: Lord, we thank You that You can always bring good things out of bad situations. Help us to remember to trust You when something bad happens to us. In Jesus' name we pray, amen.

Recommended Extras

Superbook: Paul and Silas – an animated video from the updated Superbook series, includes time-traveling children who learn lessons from the story

Paul and Silas are in Jail – free coloring and activity pages

> http://freesundayschoolcurriculum.weebly.com/upload
> s/1/2/5/0/12503916/lesson_83_paul_and_silas_are_in
> _jail.pdf

Reading the Bible for Yourself!

Use this children's Sunday School lesson to show students the importance of personally studying the Bible.

Needed: Bibles, candy

Intro Game: Telephone – Whisper a simple message in one student's ear and have them whisper the message to the next person. Students pass the message along as best they can until it reaches the last person. The last person says the message out loud to see if it matches the original message. Start with a simple message and work up to something more complex.

Lesson: Read Acts 17:10.

"As soon as it was night, the believers sent Paul and Silas away to Berea. On arriving there, they went to the Jewish synagogue."

When Paul and Silas got to the town of Berea, where did they go? (They went to the Jewish synagogue.)

What do you think a synagogue is?

"Synagogue" means "church." Paul and Silas went to the Jewish church.

Why do you think Paul and Silas went to the church? What were they doing there? (Paul and Silas went to the church to tell the people there about Jesus.)

(Read Acts 17:11.)

"Now the Berean Jews were of more noble character than those in Thessalonica, for they received the message with great eagerness and examined the Scriptures every day to see if what Paul said was true."

The Bible says that the people in that church in Berea were of noble character. What does it mean for someone to be of noble character? (It means that they do the right thing.)

And what was the right thing that the people in the church in Berea were doing?

They received Paul and Silas' message with great eagerness. That means that they believed in Jesus when Paul and Silas told them about Him. And they examined the Scriptures every day to see if what Paul said was true. That means that when Paul and Silas told them about Jesus, they went home and read their Bibles to make sure Paul and Silas were telling them the right thing.

When your Sunday School teacher or the pastor tells you something, do you go home and read your Bible to check if it's true, to check if what they told you was right?

We should all be reading the Bible for ourselves, not simply waiting and letting other people tell us about it. When a Sunday School teacher or a pastor tells us something in church, it's kind of like playing the game Telephone. We're hearing the message from someone else, not the original source.

The Bible is the original source, and the Sunday School teacher or the pastor is simply telling you what they heard from the Bible. Maybe they didn't hear it right. Maybe they forgot part of it and didn't tell you the whole thing. That's why you should go back to the original source, the Bible, and read the original message for yourself. That way, you'll know if other people are telling you the right thing or not.

(Read Acts 17:12.)

"As a result, many of them believed, as did also a number of prominent Greek women and many Greek men."

Game: Musical Chair Share – Play Musical Chairs. Remove one chair. When the music stops, the person without a chair must say one true thing about themselves. Remove no more chairs. No one leaves the game. Play until interest fades. When the game is over, explain that the Bible is like the game students just played. They told true things about themselves in the game, and the Bible is the place where God tells us true things about Himself.

Game: Sword Drill – Explain that the Bible calls the Bible a sword because it is our weapon to fight the devil. If we know what the Bible says, we will be able to defeat the devil when he tries to tempt us to do bad things. So, to start learning how to use our sword and how to read the Bible for ourselves, we're going to play a game called Sword Drill.

The teacher will call out the name of a book in the Bible and students race to get there the fastest. The first to find the book gets a piece of candy. Students who can't read can be paired up with older students, and both receive a piece of candy if they win. Students who are having trouble may be assisted by the teacher or by another student. Play as long as seems appropriate.

If your students are doing well, you can make the game harder by listing a chapter and verse or a person in the Bible instead of the name of the book only.

Closing Prayer: Father, thank You for giving us Your Word, the Bible. Help us to be like the Bereans and study the Bible for ourselves so that we can know what it says and follow it for ourselves. In Jesus' name we pray, amen.

Shipwreck!

Use this children's Sunday School lesson teach students about God's protection.

Needed: Bibles, wads of paper, index cards with the names of various animals written on them

Lesson: Tell students, Remember that in the Bible times and in other countries still today, it was against the law to believe in Jesus. It was against the law to be a Christian. And that's why many Christians were arrested and put in jail and sometimes even killed. One time when Paul was arrested—and it was actually the last time he was arrested before he died—they had to take him on a ship to Rome so that he could go to court and be judged by the Emperor, the King of Rome.

(Read Acts 27:9-20.)

"Much time had been lost, and sailing had already become dangerous because by now it was after the Day of Atonement. So Paul warned them, 'Men, I can see that our voyage is going to be disastrous and bring great loss to ship and cargo, and to our own lives also' But the centurion, instead of listening to what Paul said, followed the advice of the pilot and of the owner of the ship. Since the harbor was unsuitable to winter in, the majority decided that we should sail on, hoping to reach Phoenix and winter there. This was a harbor in Crete, facing both southwest and northwest.

"When a gentle south wind began to blow, they saw their opportunity; so they weighed anchor and sailed along the shore of Crete. Before very long, a wind of hurricane force, called the Northeaster, swept down from the island. The ship was caught by the storm and could not head into the wind; so we gave way to it and were driven along. As we passed to the lee of a small island called Cauda, we were hardly able to make the lifeboat secure, so the men hoisted it aboard. Then they passed ropes under the ship itself to hold it together. Because they were afraid they would run aground on the sandbars of Syrtis, they lowered the sea anchor and let the ship be driven along. We took such a violent battering from the storm that the next day they began to throw the cargo overboard. On the third day, they threw the ship's tackle overboard with their own hands. When neither sun nor stars appeared for many days and the storm continued raging, we finally gave up all hope of being saved.

Game: Bailing Out the Boat – Make an outline of a boat on the floor. Crumple a lot of paper. Divide students into two teams and set a timer for 3 minutes.

One team stands inside the boat outline. The other team is the storm. They pick up the crumpled papers and try to throw them into the boat outline. The team inside tries to bail out their boat by removing the papers.

After 3 minutes, tell everyone to stop and count how many wads of paper are inside the boat versus outside. The team with the lowest number of paper wads in their area wins.

Switch roles and play again.

Lesson Continues: Read Acts 27:21-28:1.

"After they had gone a long time without food, Paul stood up before them and said: 'Men, you should have taken my advice not to sail from Crete; then you would have spared yourselves this damage and loss. But now I urge you to keep up your courage, because not one of you will be lost; only the ship will be destroyed. Last night an angel of the God to whom I belong and whom I serve stood beside me and said, "Do not be afraid, Paul. You must stand trial before Caesar; and God has graciously given you the lives of all who sail with you." So keep up your courage, men, for I have faith in God that it will happen just as

He told me. Nevertheless, we must run aground on some island.'

"On the fourteenth night we were still being driven across the Adriatic Sea, when about midnight the sailors sensed they were approaching land. They took soundings and found that the water was a hundred and twenty feet deep. A short time later they took soundings again and found it was ninety feet deep. Fearing that we would be dashed against the rocks, they dropped four anchors from the stern and prayed for daylight. In an attempt to escape from the ship, the sailors let the lifeboat down into the sea, pretending they were going to lower some anchors from the bow. Then Paul said to the centurion and the soldiers, 'Unless these men stay with the ship, you cannot be saved.' So the soldiers cut the ropes that held the lifeboat and let it drift away.

"Just before dawn Paul urged them all to eat. 'For the last fourteen days,' he said, 'you have been in constant suspense and have gone without food—you haven't eaten anything. Now I urge you to take some food. You need it to survive. Not one of you will lose a single hair from his head.' After he said this, he took some bread and gave thanks to God in front of them all. Then he broke it and began to eat. They were all encouraged and ate some food themselves. Altogether there were 276 of us on board. When they had eaten as much as they wanted, they lightened the ship by throwing the grain into the sea.

"When daylight came, they did not recognize the land, but they saw a bay with a sandy beach, where they decided to run the ship aground if they could. Cutting loose the anchors, they left them in the sea and at the same time untied the ropes that held the rudders. Then they hoisted the foresail to the wind and made for the beach. But the ship struck a sandbar and ran aground. The bow stuck fast and would not move, and the stern was broken to pieces by the pounding of the surf.

"The soldiers planned to kill the prisoners to prevent any of them from swimming away and escaping. But the centurion wanted to spare Paul's life and kept them from carrying out their plan. He ordered those who could swim to jump overboard first and get to land. The rest were to get there on planks or on other pieces of the ship. In this way everyone reached land safely.

"Once safely on shore, we found out that the island was called Malta."

If you were out on the ocean and your boat got stuck, and you didn't have any food or water, what would you do?

What if your boat started breaking apart? Would that be scary?

All of the men with Paul were very scared because they thought they might drown, but God helped them all get to the beach.

Why do you think God kept Paul from drowning in the storm? (God wanted Paul to go to court and see the Emperor so that he could tell the Emperor about Jesus.)

Do you think God wants you to tell people about Jesus too? (Yes.)

God wants us all to tell people about Jesus so that they can believe in Jesus and go to Heaven when they die.

(Read Acts 28:2-6.)

"The islanders showed us unusual kindness. They built a fire and welcomed us all because it was raining and cold. Paul gathered a pile of brushwood and, as he put it on the fire, a viper, driven out by the heat, fastened itself on his hand. When the islanders saw the snake hanging from his hand, they said to each other, 'This man must be a murderer; for though he escaped from the sea, the goddess Justice has not allowed him to live.' But Paul shook the snake off into the fire and suffered no ill effects. The people expected him to swell up or suddenly fall dead; but after waiting a long time and seeing nothing unusual happen to him, they changed their minds and said he was a god."

Why do you think Paul didn't die when the snake bit him? (God protected him.)

Do you think God could protect you like He protected Paul from dying in the storm and from dying from the snake bite? (Yes.)

God can always protect us. But we have to remember that God doesn't always protect us. People do get hurt, and people do die. God can protect us, but sometimes, He won't decide to.

Game: Picking Up the Snake – Write the names of various animals on index cards and mix all the cards up facedown. When you say, "Go!" all the students pick up one of the cards and flips it over. Everyone chases the student with the snake card. Once someone tags them, mix up the cards and play again.

(Read Acts 28:7-10.)

"There was an estate nearby that belonged to Publius, the chief official of the island. He welcomed us to his home and showed us generous hospitality for three days. His father was sick in bed, suffering from fever and dysentery. Paul went in to see him and, after prayer, placed his hands on him and healed him. When this had happened, the rest of the sick on the island came and were cured. They honored us in many ways; and when we were ready to sail, they furnished us with the supplies we needed."

How do you think Paul was able to heal the man who was sick? (God gave Paul the power to heal him.)

Do you think God can give you that kind of power? (Yes.)

But again, we have to remember that God doesn't always give us that kind of power. Sometimes, He doesn't want us to be healers like Paul was. Sometimes, God simply wants us to believe in Him and do the right things in our life without doing any miracles like that. It's up to God if He gives us the power to heal or not, but He always gives us the power to resist the devil's temptations and to do what is right.

Game: Doctor, Doctor! – In this game of Freeze Tag, students will go to "Paul" for "healing" to get back in the game.

First, divide students into two teams. One team starts as It, chasing the other. Choose someone to be "Paul" on the team that is being chased. They can't be tagged.

Set a timer for 5 minutes. When a student is tagged, they have to pretend they're sick or injured and hop on one foot to where "Paul" is or wait for "Paul" to come to them. If they make it to "Paul" before they're tagged again, they are "healed" and continue as a normal player. If they get tagged before they can reach "Paul," they're out.

The round is over when your timer goes off or when the It team tags all the members of the opposite team before they can hop over to "Paul" for healing. Have the teams switch roles and play again.

Closing Prayer: Father God, we believe that You can protect us and give us the power to miracles if you want to. We also know that You don't always choose to do those things, so help us to have faith in You no matter what happens. In Jesus' name we pray, amen.

Recommended Extra

Paul is Safe in the Storm – free coloring and activity pages

http://freesundayschoolcurriculum.weebly.com/upload s/1/2/5/0/12503916/lesson_84_paul_is_safe_in_the_st orm.pdf

The Story of Paul's Death

Use this children's Sunday School lesson to teach kids that we don't need to be afraid of death.

Needed: Drawing paper, crayons or colored pencils

Intro Activity: Acting It Out – Divide students into groups of two or three. Give them a few minutes to think of their skit. Then, have each group act out what they think happens when someone dies.

Lesson: Ask students, Are any of you afraid to die?

Why do you think some people are afraid of death? (Suggestions could be it might hurt, we have to leave our family behind, our families will be sad, we have still have things we want to do, we don't know what it will be like, etc.)

Can you think of any reasons why someone would not be afraid to die? (They want to go to Heaven and see God, they know they'll get to see other family members who have died, etc.)

Who remembers what happened to Paul last time? (He was on a ship, and the ship got caught in a big storm and crashed.)

Why was Paul on the ship? Where was he going? (He was being taken as a prisoner to Rome so that he could go to court and be judged by the Emperor.)

What had he been arrested for? (For being a Christian and teaching about Jesus.)

Well, Paul finally did get to Rome on another ship. But when he got to Rome, he had to wait two whole years for his trial with the Emperor. He was on house arrest for two years. Does anyone know what house arrest means?

It means that Paul wasn't in jail, really. He had a house to live in, but a soldier also lived with him and made sure he didn't leave the house to try to escape. He had to stay in that house or have a soldier with him wherever he went.

And do you know what happened after those two years? There was a big fire in the city of Rome, the biggest and most important city in the world back then, the capital, the place where the Emperor lived.

The King, Emperor Nero, actually set the fires. He wanted to burn the whole city down and rebuild it to be like what he wanted. But when everyone got mad about the fire, Emperor Nero blamed the Christians for starting the fire. Most people back then didn't believe in Jesus. They were always picking on people who did believe in Jesus, and this was just one more time that they could pick on Christians, blaming them for the fire.

So, they arrested a bunch of Christians, including Peter. They put them in the Coliseum, the stadium, for everyone to watch them being killed. Some of the Christians they put in with lions, and the lions ate them. Some of them were put in with warriors, and the warriors attacked and killed them. Peter was hung upside on a cross. Then, since they already had Paul on house arrest, they brought him out and cut off his head.

But do you think Paul was afraid to die? (No.)

Paul wasn't afraid to die because he knew he'd be going to see God and Jesus when he died and that he would get to live forever in Heaven.

Paul also knew that he had done what he was supposed to do. He had done what God wanted. Ever since he believed in Jesus, he always tried to do the right things, and he had done his job of telling other people about Jesus.

If we believe in Jesus and do the things He wants us to do, we don't have to be afraid to die either. Instead, we can look forward to how great it will be to see God and to live forever in Heaven.

Nothing bad will ever happen in Heaven because God doesn't let anything bad happen in Heaven. No one will ever die again or get hurt. No one will ever be sad. No one will do anything wrong or mean. It'll be great!

So, don't be afraid to die and go to Heaven. When it's time for you to die, be brave, because you know you're going to see God, and it will be the best time you've ever had. Then, when it's time for Jesus to come back to Earth, He will bring your spirit back with Him and bring your body back to life too.

Craft: What Will It Be Like? – Give students drawing supplies and have them draw a picture of themselves going to Heaven. When they're finished, have them share their pictures and ask them what they think Heaven will be like.

Game: Resurrection Tag – Pick one student to be It. That student is Death. Pick another student to be Jesus. When Death tags someone, they fall down and lie on the ground like they're dead. Jesus can then come to tag them, and they can get back up. If Death tags Jesus, Jesus must count to three (because Jesus was dead for three days), but can then get up again. If Jesus tags Death, the round is over. Play until everyone has had a chance to be both Death and Jesus or as long as time permits.

Remind students that when we die, our spirit goes to Heaven, but Jesus will come back one day and will raise everyone who believes in Him back to life.

Closing Prayer: Father God, we thank You that we don't need to be afraid of dying because You'll bring our spirits to Heaven when we die, and Jesus will bring our bodies back to life when He comes again. We only pray that You'll help us to live how You want us to live and do the work that You want us to do until we do die. In Jesus' name we pray, amen.

Made in the USA
Monee, IL
04 December 2023

48177188R00036